I Will Not Name It

Except to Say

LEE SHARKEY

I Will Not Name It
Except to Say

TUPELO PRESS

North Adams, Massachusetts

Library of Congress Control Number:

ISBN-13: 978-1-946482-49-5

Cover image: *Angelus Novus,* monoprint by Paul Klee. Used by permission.
Cover and text design by Ann Aspell.

First paperback edition April 2021

Tupelo Press
P.O. Box 1767
North Adams, Massachusetts 01247
(413) 664-9611 / Fax: (413) 664-9711
editor@tupelopress.org / www.tupelopress.org

Tupelo Press is an award-winning independent literary press that publishes fine fiction, non-fiction, and poetry in books that are a joy to hold as well as read. Tupelo Press is a registered 501(c)(3) non-profit organization, and we rely on public support to carry out our mission of publishing extraordinary work that may be outside the realm of the large commercial publishers. Financial donations are welcome and are tax deductible.

to Martha, friend in poetry—forever

CONTENTS

I

II

The Samuel Bak Poems